How Can I Be Right with God?

Crucial Questions booklets provide a quick introduction to definitive Christian truths. This expanding collection includes titles such as:

Who Is Jesus?

Can I Trust the Bible?

Does Prayer Change Things?

Can I Know God's Will?

How Should I Live in This World?

What Does It Mean to Be Born Again?

Can I Be Sure I'm Saved?

What Is Faith?

What Can I Do with My Guilt?

What Is the Trinity?

CQ

How Can I Be Right with God?

R.C. SPROUL

Reformation Trust A DIVISION OF LIGONIER MINISTRIES, ORLANDO, FL

How Can I Be Right with God?

Published by Reformation Trust Publishing
A division of Ligonier Ministries
421 Ligonier Court, Sanford, FL 32771
Ligonier.org   ReformationTrust.com

Printed in China
RR Donnelley
0001018
First edition, third printing

ISBN 978-1-64289-061-7 (Paperback)
ISBN 978-1-64289-089-1 (ePub)
ISBN 978-1-64289-117-1 (Kindle)

Cover design: Ligonier Creative
Interior typeset: Katherine Lloyd, The DESK

Library of Congress Cataloging-in-Publication Data

Names: Sproul, R.C. (Robert Charles), 1939-2017 author.
Title: How can I be right with God? / by R.C. Sproul.
Description: Orlando, FL : Reformation Trust Publishing, 2017. | Series: Crucial questions ; No. 26 | Includes bibliographical references.
Identifiers: LCCN 2017023438 | ISBN 9781567698374
Subjects: LCSH: Justification (Christian theology) | Salvation--Christianity. | Assurance (Theology)
Classification: LCC BT764.3 .S6695 2017 | DDC 234/.7--dc23
LC record available at https://lccn.loc.gov/2017023438

Contents

Chapter One

After Darkness, Light

In the old city of Geneva, Switzerland, there is a large park on the grounds of the University of Geneva that commemorates the Reformation. That park is adorned with a huge wall, called the International Monument to the Reformation or simply the Reformation Wall. In statues and bas-reliefs, the wall depicts figures from the Reformation including John Calvin, John Knox, William Farel, and Theodore Beza. Surrounding these and other statues, the motto of the Reformation is inscribed on each side: *post tenebras lux*—after darkness, light.

This phrase refers not only to the unveiling and liberation of the Scriptures—which were made available to the common people during the Reformation—but also to the loss and recovery of the most important biblical doctrine there is: the doctrine of justification by faith alone. This was the primary and central issue of the Protestant Reformation. During the dispute between the Protestants and the Roman Catholics, both sides saw that justification was so important that no compromise was possible. Both sides were convinced that what was at stake in the doctrine of justification was the very essence of the biblical gospel. When the gospel is at stake, everything is at stake, because the gospel tells us how we can be right with God.

In Galatians 1:6–9, Paul writes about the importance of getting the gospel right:

> I am astonished that you are so quickly deserting him who called you in the grace of Christ and are turning to a different gospel—not that there is another one, but there are some who trouble you and want to distort the gospel of Christ. But even

> if we or an angel from heaven should preach to you a gospel contrary to the one we preached to you, let him be accursed. As we have said before, so now I say again: If anyone is preaching to you a gospel contrary to the one you received, let him be accursed.

This Apostle was a man who was constantly extolling the virtues of patience, gentleness, meekness, charity, and tolerance; who, conversely, constantly rebuked the sins of contentiousness, divisiveness, quarrelsome spirits, belligerence, and so on. This man said that we ought to strive as much as we possibly can to live at peace with all men; he was known as the Apostle of peace and unity. Yet suddenly he came to a point over a doctrine where he said, "There can be no toleration here. To tolerate the distortion of the gospel into another gospel is to tolerate the intolerable."

The first thing that Paul did was express his amazement—not that the people had left the gospel that he had preached to them, but that they had done it so quickly. He was hardly gone from their midst before they wanted to listen to the teachings of the Judaizers, who insisted that one cannot be saved by faith in Christ alone but must also have good works and obedience to the law in order to be saved. This "other gospel" was no gospel at all—there is only one gospel, the gospel of God, revealed in and through Christ and proclaimed and expounded by the Apostles. The stakes are so high when it comes to this point that Paul pronounced a curse on anyone who teaches otherwise. The Greek work translated "accursed" is *anathema*—damned.

The Apostle understood that the issue of justification was no mere academic issue, but one that touches every person's life ultimately. It can be summed up in one question: How are we saved? It is a life-and-death matter, an eternal life matter. The New Testament makes it clear that each of us will be called into account before God, and that God is righteous while we're not. The doctrine of justification addresses the solution to that problem, declaring how we, as unjust people, can be reconciled to a just and holy God. So if there's anything in the essence of the Christian faith, of the good news of the gospel, it's this doctrine.

Martin Luther, building on Paul's assessment, called the doctrine of justification the article on which the church stands or falls. Luther understood that theology is systematic, and that a distortion of the gospel will influence and affect everything else that we believe in the Christian faith. John Calvin said something very similar: "We must so discuss [justification by faith] as to bear in mind that this is the main hinge on which religion turns, so that we devote the greater attention and care to it. For unless you first of all grasp what your relationship to God is, and the nature of his judgment concerning you, you have neither a foundation on which to establish your salvation nor one on which to build piety toward God."*

Do you think it's important to know how you can be saved? Does it matter to you what is the basis upon which your own salvation rests? I can't think of anything that matters more. We must all ask, with the Philippian jailer, "What must I do to be saved?" (Acts 16:30).

* *Institutes of the Christian Religion* 3.11.1.

Chapter Two

Luther's Discovery

Martin Luther had a reputation among his fellow monks as being strange. His behavior in the confessional was notorious: he would go into daily confession and spend an hour, two hours, sometimes four hours confessing his sins, until his confessor would become frustrated and wonder if Luther was simply trying to shirk his duties. He would confess the smallest transgressions, prompting the brothers to say, "If you're going to confess a sin, confess one that's significant; don't keep us in here for hours reciting these peccadilloes." But Luther was sincere; he really was tormented, and he would get peace for a few moments when the priest gave him absolution. Then he would leave the confessional, go back to his cell, and be plunged into despair because he remembered a sin that he had forgotten to mention in the confessional. Because of this torment over his guilt, some have even suggested that he was mentally unbalanced.

If we look beyond his confessional practices, we see that Luther's entire life was marked by one crisis after another. It seemed that these crises came about every five years. In 1505, Luther was studying law and had already distinguished himself as one of the leading thinkers in the field of jurisprudence in all of Europe. If we want to understand Luther's theological torment, we have to recognize that he brought an expert's legal mind to the law of God. When he examined the law of God, he was driven to the edge of despair because he realized that his life never measured up to the radical demands of purity and holiness that he found there. At one point, he said, "You ask me if I love God. Love God? Sometimes I hate Him!" He saw God as an angry judge who applies the measuring stick of the absolute law of God to his performance, and Luther knew he came up short.

On one occasion in 1505 when he was on his way home from university, a fierce storm suddenly arose and a lightning bolt struck next to him. He was thrown from his horse and almost killed. In panic, he cried out: "Help me, Saint Anne! I will become a monk." To his father's consternation, Luther left his legal studies and entered the Augustinian monastery at Wittenberg to fulfill his vow.

In 1510, Luther had a second major crisis. He had been sent to Rome to act as a delegate to a convocation of his order. Luther was elated to have been selected; at that time in church history, making sacred pilgrimages had great value in terms of penance, so making a pilgrimage to the holy city would allow Luther to gain some merit for his soul. In Rome, the cradle of the church, he hoped to find the peace that he was longing for. However, when he arrived in the Eternal City, he was shocked. He witnessed visible corruption of the clergy, sexual corruption that had been unprecedented in the history of the church, and fellow priests running through the Mass in five minutes just to get it done. He didn't see any sense of piety or devotion to the things of God.

At the heart of his pilgrimage, Luther was to go to the sacred steps—allegedly the steps that Jesus walked after leaving His hearing before Pontius Pilate. They had been brought from Jerusalem and installed in Rome. Pilgrims would come and climb these stairs on their knees, saying the rosary as they went. And so Luther went, climbing these stone stairs. He said a prayer on each step, kissing each one, all the way to the top. As he got to the top, he was struck with the thought that maybe it didn't work, and he said aloud, "Who knows if it is true?" Thus, Luther's visit to Rome, which he had hoped would rid him of his doubts and torment, only exacerbated his anguish.

His third major crisis took place in 1515. Luther was by then a doctor of the church and was teaching theology and biblical studies at the University of Wittenberg. He had recently finished a series of lectures on the book of Psalms and was about to begin a series on Paul's letter to the Romans. While he was preparing for those lectures, he studied the verse in which Paul, introducing the theme of justification, said, "For in it the righteousness of God is revealed from faith for faith, as it is written, 'The righteous shall live by faith'" (Rom. 1:17). Luther naturally assumed that when it spoke about the righteousness of God, it was referring to God's own intrinsic, inherent righteousness. This was the thing Luther feared most in all the world, because he knew that he was not righteous and God was. He couldn't see much good news in a gospel that reveals the righteousness of God to people who aren't righteous.

During the course of his preparations, Luther read some works by the patron of his order, Augustine of Hippo. On Romans 1:17, Augustine wrote: "He does not say, the righteousness of man, or the righteousness of his own will, but the 'righteousness *of God*,'—not that whereby He is Himself righteous, but that with which He endows man when He justifies the ungodly."* Luther said that, as he understood this insight from Augustine, light flooded his soul: "Thereupon I felt myself to be reborn and to have gone through open doors into paradise."** He had a profound existential experience where the burden of his unresolved guilt rolled off his back, and he realized that the only way he could stand before a just and holy God was to be cloaked in the righteousness of Christ, which Luther couldn't beg, borrow, steal, deserve, or earn, but could only humbly receive.

When you look at the Reformation, there is a sense in which Martin Luther stood *contra mundum*—against

---

* Augustine of Hippo, *A Treatise on the Spirit and the Letter*, chap. 16.

** Roland Bainton, *Here I Stand* (Nashville, Tenn.: Abingdon, 1950), 50.

the world. A man has to be unbelievably insubordinate, arrogant, or crazy to defy all of the authorities that Luther defied and refuse to budge from his position. Certainly, Luther was a stubborn man, but even the most stubborn of men ought to have been worn down by the relentless critique that he received from the authorities. Why wouldn't he back down? He had fought too hard and long to gain peace with God to surrender to anyone. It was in that experience in his study that his conviction of justification by faith alone was awakened, and when he came to the rest of Romans after that insight from Augustine, the clarity of Paul's teaching on the doctrine steeled Luther such that he wouldn't negotiate it with anyone for any earthly reason.

I don't think Martin Luther was crazy. I think he was perhaps the most honest Christian who ever lived after the first century. He understood something about the character of God, the righteousness of God, and the justness of God—and the more we understand how righteous God is, the less we can deceive ourselves about our lack of righteousness. We tend to evaluate ourselves by our own standard, hoping that God will grade us all on a curve. If we think He can find someone who's more wicked than we are, we take solace or refuge in that, and we don't focus on the standard by which we are to be judged.

But Luther saw that God's standard is not a sliding scale; it is His own perfect righteousness. It was at that moment that Luther realized that the only righteousness that could ever save him could not come from himself; it had to come from God. At that moment, the seeds of the Reformation germinated.

There have been times in my life where I have been afflicted by melancholy. Particularly as a young student and a budding theologian, I used to find myself feeling depressed about things and discouraged. When I found myself in such a place, I would turn to Luther—not because I was looking for theological insights that I couldn't find somewhere else, but because I could identify with him. He was so earthy. He had to fight these things all the time. He talked about having an ongoing, endless struggle with Satan himself where Satan would come at him with what Luther called an *Anfechtung*—an unbridled assault against him to take away his joy, his peace, and his comfort. Luther said that at such times he would rush to the gospel and rest upon it in order to refresh his understanding of the peace with God that was his in Christ. Luther embodied the struggle of every Christian to have peace with God, and in his victory we too can see the path to hope that is found in Christ.

Chapter Three

God's Legal Declaration

When we consider justification, we are concerned with something that has to do with justice. Thus, we have a legal concern. As people who are created in the image of God, we are destined to stand before the judgment seat of God. Jesus taught that there will be a time when every idle word spoken will be brought into judgment; the secret things will be made plain, and we will all be assembled before the tribunal of God. The problem that we face is twofold: God Himself is absolutely holy and just in His character and being, yet we have all fallen short of the glory of God—so we are unjust. The fundamental question is: How can an unjust person survive the judgment of a just and holy God? As David put it: "If you, O Lord, should mark iniquities, O Lord, who could stand?" (Ps. 130:3). Obviously, the answer to that rhetorical question is that no one could possibly stand before a judgment that requires perfection—and if God counts our sins, we most certainly will fail in this judgment. So the problem for every human being who has ever sinned is the problem of becoming justified in order to survive the judgment of God.

Luther and the Reformers understood the biblical teaching of justification in terms of *forensic* justification. You've probably heard of court testimony regarding forensic evidence; you may have heard of forensic medicine or forensic science, meaning it has to do with a legal environment—a court setting. There's another way in which you might have heard the term *forensic* in more ordinary language. When I was in high school, one of the clubs we had was the debate club, and every year they would compete in a statewide competition called a forensics tournament. It involved exercises in debate, public speaking, and that sort of thing. The word was used to describe various kinds of oratory, and so *forensics* in that sense had to do with making declarations and arguments for or against something.

If we tie together these two ways of using the term *forensic*—one with respect to the law courts and one with respect to public speaking—we get close to the way the term *forensic* is used in theology, that is, with respect to legal declarations. Thus, *forensic justification* means that justification rests upon some kind of legal declaration. In the simplest terms, that means that justification takes place when God declares a person to be just in His sight. If God says, "You are just," then you have been justified.

Even though the Reformed doctrine of justification by faith alone is generally referred to as forensic justification, there's a subtle point here that we must not miss. The Roman Catholic view of justification, as radically different as it is from the Protestant view, nevertheless agrees at this point—namely, that ultimately justification takes place when God declares a person just. But the Roman church doesn't see this declaration in the same way that the Reformers understood it, because the fundamental issue in the Reformation concerned the basis upon which God declares an unjust person to be just.

Martin Luther used a famous phrase to summarize his understanding of forensic justification: *simul justus et peccator*, meaning "at the same time just and sinner." At first blush, this sounds like a contradiction, but it isn't. A contradiction exists when we say that something is one thing and something else at the same time and in the same sense or in the same relationship. Luther was saying that indeed, the justified person is at one and the same time just and sinner, but he wasn't saying that we are in the same sense just and sinner or in the same relationship just and sinner. We are just in one sense and sinner in another sense. If we grasp this, we penetrate quickly to the heart of the Reformation in its concern about the doctrine of justification by faith alone.

In simple terms, what Luther meant is this: The good news of the gospel is that we don't have to wait until we become perfectly righteous *in ourselves* before God will consider us and declare us righteous or accept us in His sight as justified people. God makes a provision for justification whereby people who are sinners, while they are still sinners, can be reconciled to Him and declared just in His sight. So Luther's point was that justification by faith alone means that a person who is justified is in one sense perfectly righteous and in another sense still a sinner. This raises the question: In what sense are we righteous, and in what sense are we sinners?

We are made and declared righteous by virtue of God's imputing to us the righteousness of Christ, of His counting Jesus' righteousness and merit for us. We are just by virtue of Christ's righteousness—but if God were to consider us in and of ourselves, in our naked humanity, without seeing us in Christ, He would find us to be sinners. We are not miraculously changed into sinless people; we are sinners in the process of becoming sanctified. We are, in Luther's terms, people who have a medical condition and have been given medicine, which takes time to cure us. But we don't have to wait for God to accept us in Christ. So this forensic declaration is based upon a transfer or accounting: Christ's righteousness and merit are attributed to us while we are still sinners.

The Roman Catholic Church objects to the phrase *simul justus et peccator* and to the idea of God's declaring someone to be just who is still a sinner. The church says it casts a shadow on the integrity or honesty of God. How can God call someone just who's not just? How can God regard as righteous a person who is, in fact, a sinner? The

Roman Catholic authorities argued that for God to do such a thing would be for Him to involve Himself in a kind of legal fiction. The Reformers responded that it's not a legal fiction, it's a legal diction. It is a legal judgment, decree, and declaration. What makes it true and not fictional is that God makes a real transfer of actual righteousness to our account.

A common misunderstanding is that the only thing that Jesus did to save people was to die on the cross for their sins, and that's certainly very important to our justification. But if all it took for people to be justified was for Christ to pay the penalty due for sin, then He would have descended from heaven fully grown, gone directly to the cross to pay the price and satisfy the demands of God's justice, then returned in glory to heaven with His people's redemption accomplished. In biblical terms, however, two things are required. The first is that our sin must be punished, which Christ's death on the cross accomplished. But all that did was get us back to a state of innocence, like Adam before the fall. We would still have no positive righteousness to bring before God. So the second thing that is required to effect our redemption is that there must be a provision of positive righteousness for God to declare us righteous. That's why Christ came into the world born as a baby, born under the law, in order to become the new Adam and to live His entire life in perfect, active obedience before God. For Jesus to qualify as our Savior, He had to live a sinless life in addition to dying an atoning death.

What happens in our justification is that a double imputation takes place. To impute is to transfer or credit, so our sins are imputed to Jesus and His righteousness is imputed to us. Both sides are necessary for our salvation—the negative payment for sin and the positive achievement of real righteousness.

When Luther said we are at the same time just and sinner, he meant that we are just by virtue of the transfer of the righteousness of Christ to our account legally while we still have the remains of sin in our lives. The basis or the ground of our justification, by which God declares us just, is not because He looks at us and sees our righteousness, but because He sees the righteousness of Christ.

Forensic justification involves a legal declaration by God. Thus, when Luther said the doctrine of justification by faith alone is the article upon which the church stands or falls, it is plain to see that it's the article upon which any of us stands or falls. Again, the words of David point to this: "If you, O LORD, should mark iniquities, O Lord who could stand?" (Ps. 130:3). The implication is that none of us could possibly stand if God counted our sins and treated us objectively strictly on the sin that He finds in our lives.

The question for you is: How do you hope to stand before the judgment seat of God? Maybe you're hoping that there will never be a time of reckoning, accountability, or evaluation, or you're hoping that God will grade you on a curve and will think that you have lived a "good enough" life even though you haven't lived a perfect life. Upon what are you depending to pass that test? If you're depending upon your own righteousness, you should despair of that this day because it most certainly will fail you. You must have a righteousness that belongs to someone else if you are to pass the bar of God's exam—and there's only one person whose righteousness is sufficient: Jesus Christ.

Chapter Four

The Great Exchange

Imagine three circles drawn on a blackboard. The first circle represents God; the second represents Jesus. The third circle on the blackboard represents human beings, or the sinner—us. If I were to take chalk and put marks inside the first circle to represent the evil or sins or even defects that are found in the character of God, how many marks would I put in it? Absolutely none, because God is perfectly holy and perfectly righteous. It would be blasphemous for me to mar His character with my chalk. Now, considering Jesus, how many indications of sin would I put in that circle? Again, zero.

Christianity Today once reported on a poll that was taken among professing evangelicals, the majority of whom said that man is basically good. Nobody's perfect, but apparently most believe that whatever sin we have is not of the essence, not something that penetrates to the root of our being. So, maybe what I should do with the circle that represents mankind is put a couple of blemishes, just a couple of little dots in the circle. We might even be convicted enough to put a little bit more—but to keep it on the edge of the circle, making sure that the shading doesn't penetrate to the center, lest we suggest that there's something fundamentally wrong with the human character.

But does that half-shaded circle do justice to what the Scriptures say? The Bible says, "The LORD saw that the wickedness of man was great in the earth, and that every intention of the thoughts of his heart was only evil continually" (Gen. 6:5), and, "None is righteous, no, not one; no one understands; no one seeks for God" (Rom. 3:10–11). Most Christians might want to shade in most of this circle, but most of them would leave one portion undisturbed—a little island of righteousness that is not affected by the fall.

But the teaching of Reformed theology is that the circle representing humankind should be filled in completely.

The reason for imagining these circles is so that we can have a visual understanding of the imputation of Christ's righteousness. Before we come back to these circles, let's turn our attention to Paul's teaching in the fourth chapter of Romans:

> What then shall we say was gained by Abraham, our forefather according to the flesh? For if Abraham was justified by works, he has something to boast about, but not before God. For what does the Scripture say? "Abraham believed God, and it was counted to him as righteousness." Now to the one who works, his wages are not counted as a gift but as his due. And to the one who does not work but believes in him who justifies the ungodly, his faith is counted as righteousness, just as David also speaks of the blessing of the one to whom God counts righteousness apart from works: "Blessed are those whose lawless deeds are forgiven, and whose sins are covered; blessed is the man against whom the Lord will not count his sin." (Rom. 4:1–8)

It wasn't Martin Luther or John Calvin who invented the idea of the imputation of righteousness. This concept is deeply and firmly rooted in Scripture itself, both in the Old and New Testaments. When Paul gave his exposition of the gospel and the doctrine of justification, he appealed to the Old Testament—specifically to Abraham, going back to Genesis 15, where God made a promise of redemption to Abraham, and Abraham believed that promise. The Scriptures tell us in Genesis 15 that God counted Abraham as righteous the moment he believed the promise of God. The point Paul is making in Romans 4 is that before Abraham did a single work—before he obeyed anything that God commanded, before he was circumcised, before he kept any of the law of God—God pronounced him just. Abraham was a sinner, yet the moment he believed, God counted Abraham as righteous in His sight by faith. God forensically considered Abraham to be something that he was not yet in himself: righteous.

The idea of imputation is mentioned more than once in this text. In verses 2 through 4, Paul says, "For if Abraham was justified by works, he has something to boast about, but not before God. For what does the Scripture say? 'Abraham believed God, and it was counted to him as righteousness.' Now to the one who works, his wages are not counted as a gift but as his due." The "counting" of Abraham as righteous refers to the imputation of righteousness. God imputed this righteousness to Abraham freely, that is, not under compulsion. It was not as if God owed it to Abraham or was indebted to him. Simply on the basis of His pure grace, God announced and proclaimed Abraham to be just in His sight. Paul elaborates on this in verses 5 and 6: "And to the one who does not work but believes in him who justifies the ungodly, his faith is counted as righteousness, just as David also speaks of the blessing of the one to whom God counts righteousness apart from works." I don't know how the Apostle could have put it more plainly: God imputes righteousness to people apart from works. That's what Luther's *simul justus et peccator* is about. Then it is stated in both affirmative and negative terms in verses 7 and 8: "Blessed are those whose lawless deeds are forgiven, and whose sins are covered; blessed is the man against whom the Lord will not count his sin."

In justification, two kinds of imputation take place: there is the imputation of the righteousness of Christ to us and the imputation of our sin to Christ. The second kind of imputation carries with it also a kind of non-imputation: God does *not* impute something to us, namely, our sin. In simple language, God counts the righteousness of Christ *for* us, and does not count our own sins *against* us. That is good news! Could there possibly be any better news than God's saying that He will not only provide us with Christ's righteousness, but also will not hold our sins against us?

Going back to the circles on the blackboard, remember that the first circle—representing God—has no blemish in it. Likewise, the second, representing Jesus, has no blemish. But the third circle, for you, me, and all of mankind, is filled in from the core to its edges. What happened on the cross? What does the New Testament mean when it teaches that Jesus is our sin-bearer? John the Baptist heralded Christ when he saw Him: "Behold, the Lamb of God, who takes away the sin of the world!" (John 1:29). How does Jesus take away our sin? How does the cross have any significance for me? Why did God, who is perfect and just, pour out His wrath upon Jesus, who in and of Himself was sinless—perfectly innocent—in the life He lived on earth? The only way God can be exonerated for pouring His wrath upon Christ is if Christ really, truly took upon Himself our sin, transgressions, and guilt. The taking of our guilt upon Himself involves an imputation. When Christ went to the cross, He was saying to the Father, "Father, count their sins against Me. Let Me stand in their place and act on behalf of My people as their vicarious representative. Lay the sins of Your people, O God, upon Me." This involved a legal transfer, a reckoning—an imputation.

In the second circle representing Jesus, there's not a single blemish before the cross. But on the cross, how many blemishes were on Jesus? All of our sin was transferred to His account, and so the sin moved from us to Him; in God's sight, Christ was covered with our sins. Our sins are imputed to Christ; He suffered the real punishment of God's wrath and justice for our sins. But this is only half of the transaction—it's not enough for our unrighteousness to be transferred to Jesus' account. Christ took the penalty for our sin, but we still have sin in our lives. The circle representing us would still be filled with chalk. But the metaphor that Scripture uses is a covering—a cloak is put over our sin. Our sin is covered by the righteousness of Christ, the merit that He earned by His perfectly obedient life. When God looks at us, He sees the righteousness of Christ; the Bible says Christ is "our righteousness" (Jer.

33:16). The ground or basis on which we are declared just by God is the justice, righteousness, or merit of Christ.

One of the slogans of the Reformation was *sola fide*, meaning that justification is by "faith alone." That was simply shorthand for a much more profound concept. What justification by faith alone really means is that justification is by Christ alone—by the righteousness of Jesus Christ, whose righteousness is the only righteousness in the universe that is enough, that has enough merit to satisfy the demands of the justice of God. This is what Paul summarized in Romans 4: the twofold blessedness. We are blessed because our sin is not counted to us but imputed to Christ, and His righteousness is imputed to us by God's forensic decree. As we will see, the only way that happens is by faith.

What do you suppose would happen to you if, when you came to the judgment seat of God, God gave you a piece of chalk and said, "Now I want you to fill in every time you've ever sinned, every time you've sinned in thought, word, or deed. Anytime you've fallen short of My commandments, I want you to put a mark in your circle"? How much chalk would you need? I don't think there's enough chalk in heaven that would enable me to give a perfect account of my imperfection. No wonder the New Testament describes

Christ's coming in judgment as it does: people who are not ready will cry out for the mountains to fall upon them and the hills to cover them. What we need more than anything else when we stand before God is a covering—something that will blot out our transgressions. That's what the gospel promises to give to all who believe: the covering of the righteousness of Christ.

Chapter Five

The Means of Salvation

We've seen that the New Testament view of our justification is based upon the righteousness of Christ that is transferred, reckoned, or imputed to us. Scripture speaks of this imputation as happening by faith. This does not mean that faith itself is so meritorious that it makes up for all sins. It is vital that we be careful not to turn faith into a thinly veiled work, misunderstanding justification by faith to mean that someone is justified in the sight of God because "he has faith" and thus he is righteous because he has done a work of believing. That is not what the New Testament means, nor was it what the Reformers meant, when speaking of justification that is by faith.

Sometimes the word *by* can be translated as "through." It refers to the means by which something is accomplished. Thus, the way "by faith" functions in the New Testament is as the means or the instrument by which justification happens. That may seem harmless enough, but this word *instrument* or *instrumental* was very much a part of the controversy in the sixteenth century with respect to justification.

The ancient philosopher Aristotle had a tremendous influence on all of Western philosophy and was highly respected in traditional Christian circles. He tried to analyze the whole process of causality with careful scrutiny. Sometimes people are less than precise, particularly when our children ask, "Why did such-and-such happen?" Wanting to avoid detailed explanations, the answer might be, "Because." The word *because* has to do with causality. Aristotle said there are different contributing factors that bring about certain events or effects, and he distinguished among several types of causes.

To use an illustration that Aristotle used, imagine a

sculptor who fashions a magnificent statue out of a raw piece of stone. What causes that statue? Aristotle said we can name different causes. First, there's the material cause: this is the stuff out of which something is produced, without which you can't have that something. In this case, if there is no stone, there can be no statue, so the material cause of that statue is the block of stone with which the artist started. Second, there is the efficient cause: this is the thing that brings about an effect. The stone doesn't make itself into a statue; something else has to be there besides the stone. The efficient cause in this case is the sculptor who does the work of transforming the bare block of stone into a statue. Next, Aristotle spoke of the formal cause: this is the blueprint or idea. The artist started off with an idea in his mind or a sketch on a piece of paper. It's this plan that guided his thinking and his work as he progressed in shaping the block of stone into the statue. There is also the instrumental cause: this is the means by which the efficient cause brings about an effect. In this case, it is the hammer, chisel, and other tools or instruments by which the sculptor does his work. The final cause is the end for the thing in question, the purpose for which it is done. When it comes to the sculpture, the sculptor may have been commissioned to produce a statue for a king's garden, or perhaps he did it for his own enjoyment.

The instrumental cause of justification was a hotly contested issue in the sixteenth century because the Protestant Reformers and the Roman Catholic theologians did not agree—and still don't—on what the instrumental cause of our justification is. The Roman Catholic Church declared at the Council of Trent in the sixteenth century that the instrumental cause of justification is baptism, at least initially. In baptism, justifying grace—the grace of the righteousness of Christ—is infused into the soul so that the recipient now has the grace of Christ poured into his soul. Now that person has been cleansed of original sin and is in a state of justifying grace because of the grace that inhabits him. This inhabiting grace can be augmented or diminished; it can increase or decrease or even be lost altogether.

The recipient of baptism is in a state of grace and possesses the grace of justification. He is in good shape unless or until he commits a mortal sin. The Roman Catholic Church historically has distinguished between two kinds of sin: mortal and venial. Venial sin is really sin, but it's less serious than mortal sin, which is so egregious, so heinous, so destructive, so wicked that it kills something: the infused grace of justification. That's why, if a person commits mortal sin, he loses his justification and has to be justified again.

It is at that point that the second instrumental cause of justification comes in: penance. The Council of Trent defined penance as "the second plank" of justification for those who have made "shipwreck of their souls." It allows someone who has committed a mortal sin to receive a new infusion of the justifying grace of Christ and His righteousness, which keeps that person in good standing before God unless or until he again commits mortal sin, for which he can receive penance again, and so on.

To Rome, it is possible for a person to lose the grace of justification and it is also possible for him to lose his faith. If he loses his faith, he also loses his justification. But it's possible for someone to keep his faith and still lose his justification if he commits a mortal sin. So a person who still possesses true faith can be outside the state of grace, not in a state of justification; he would need to be restored to that state through penance.

The Roman Catholic Church considers the sacraments of baptism and penance the instrumental causes of justification because they are the vehicles through which, or the means by which, justifying grace is given or communicated to the individual. When such grace is given, it is infused into the recipient, but it must meet with a particular response. The recipient must cooperate with this infused grace and assent to it in order for it to produce real righteousness.

In the Reformed view, the righteousness of Christ is imputed by faith to the believer. For the Roman Catholic Church, the righteousness of Christ is infused into someone by the sacraments, and that person must then cooperate with this infusion of grace in order to become truly, inherently righteous.

This dispute about the means, or the instrumental cause, focused on the phrase *justification by faith alone.* What Luther and Calvin meant by that phrase was this: When the New Testament speaks of our being justified by faith, the instrumental cause of our justification—the tool or means by which we are justified—is not the sacraments but faith and faith alone. Faith is the instrument by which we are linked to the righteousness of Christ. It's the conduit through which His righteousness is given to us. The minute someone has faith, he receives through it the righteousness of Christ and is justified.

It's important to note that the Roman church agrees with the Protestants that the work of Christ is absolutely essential for our salvation. It has repeatedly condemned the ancient Pelagian heresy that a person could be justified in the sight of God strictly on the basis of his own exercise of his will, performance, and works, apart from God's grace.

That wasn't the issue in the sixteenth century. The basic issue was, how does the objective work of Christ become ours? How is the work that Christ performed, without which no one could be saved, appropriated to the individual believer? The Roman Catholic Church saw that it was appropriated fundamentally through the sacraments and this cooperative venture that we're involved in, whereas the Reformers taught that it was appropriated simply and completely by faith alone.

Chapter Six

By Christ Alone

In the sixth session of the Council of Trent, the Roman Catholic Church defined its doctrine of justification, giving a list of more than twenty canons of denunciation—views that they repudiated, including the Reformation view. But in their exposition of the doctrine of justification, the church decreed that faith is necessary for justification.

Some say that the Roman Catholic Church thinks that faith is insignificant, unimportant, or unnecessary. One of the worst slanders against the Roman Catholic Church is that the difference between Rome and Protestants is the Protestants believe in justification by faith, and the Catholics believe in justification by works, as if the Roman church didn't believe in the necessity of faith. That is simply not true.

In the canons of the Council of Trent, the Roman church said three fundamental things about faith as it relates to justification: faith is the initial movement; it is the foundation of justification; and it is the root of justification. Thus, the Roman Catholic Church does not teach that justification happens apart from faith because it's by faith that we enter into the sacraments and we receive the infusion of the righteousness of Christ, and it's by faith that we work with that infused grace, that we cooperate with it and assent to it so that righteousness then begins to inhere within us.

But what's missing in the Roman Catholic formula regarding faith is the word *sola*. When Luther made the declaration *sola fide*—that justification is by faith alone—that word *alone* is what provoked a lot of the controversy. The Reformers would say, in response to the Council of Trent, that faith is not only the initial step, foundation, or root of justification; it is all you need for justification to follow, that is, for a person to receive the imputation of the righteousness of Christ. The only thing we need to get the benefit of the work of Christ is faith. Anyone who has true faith immediately and completely receives all the benefits of the work of Jesus Christ. Calvin insisted that justification is not just initiated by faith, it is completed by faith. The very second someone has true faith, God declares him justified and imputes to him all of the merit of Christ, so that all that Christ is and all that He has accomplished becomes his.

Luther referred to the righteousness that justifies us as *extra nos*, meaning "outside of us." He meant that the righteousness that justifies us is not our own. He used another Latin phrase to capture this idea: *alienum iustitsia*, which means "alien righteousness." When Luther said that the justice or righteousness by which we are justified is an alien righteousness, a righteousness that is *extra nos*, he meant that the righteousness that justifies the Christian, and the only righteousness that could ever justify a Christian, is the righteousness that inherently belongs to Jesus. It's given to us and counted for us, but properly speaking, it is Jesus' own righteousness.

If indeed the righteousness by which we are justified is something already accomplished by Jesus, what the

Apostles and Reformers were saying is that the only thing for me to do to receive the benefit of that righteousness is to put my trust in it, rely upon it, grasp it in faith, receive it, and embrace it humbly, receiving this free gift of justification by relying on Jesus and Him alone. That's what is meant by justification by faith alone.

For the Roman Catholic Church, the justice by which we are justified comes from Christ initially, but it becomes ours as we cooperate with it and it becomes inherent within us so that it is properly our own justice, our own righteousness. Then it isn't alien or extra; it's inner, a righteousness that is in us, not one that is apart from us.

While the Roman Catholic Church denies the doctrine of justification by faith alone, it does not deny the importance of faith; it does not teach that justification is by works alone. But it does insist that certain works are necessary in order for a person to be deemed just by God, which can be seen most clearly in its doctrine of penance, as we saw in the last chapter.

The Roman Catholic Church does not say that a person can become righteous without Christ or without grace. It does not deny the sinner's dependence upon Jesus Christ and His grace for justification. Christ is necessary for justification, but in the sense that He makes it possible for us to be justified. If we cooperate with and assent to His grace, we actually become inherently righteous; only when that righteousness is inherent within us will God declare us just.

Luther got exercised about the idea that we could possibly have any merit or righteousness of our own that would avail before God's throne. He said the Word of God is a thunderbolt against all kinds of merit apart from the merit of Christ. The Roman church repudiated *sola fide* because it believed that a person, in addition to faith, must have works, and in addition to works, must have merit in order to be deemed just and to be rewarded by God. But the Reformers believed that this concept of work and merit cast a shadow upon the full purchase of our redemption that was accomplished once and for all by the merit of Christ that was won for us and for all who believe.

One beloved hymn of the church is "Rock of Ages" by Augustus Toplady. A verse in that hymn says, "Nothing in my hand I bring—simply to the cross I cling / Naked, come to Thee for dress; helpless, look to Thee for grace / Foul, I, to the fountain, fly—wash me, Savior, or I die." This hymn directs our attention to where we must put our reliance and confidence for salvation. It must not rest in our own activity, performance, or merit—rather, our confidence must look to Christ, who alone has sufficient merit for us, and whose righteousness is perfect and freely given to all who put their trust in Him. The only merit that we bring to the judgment seat of God of our own is demerit.

Chapter Seven

The Essentials of Biblical Faith

If justification is by faith, then we must come to an understanding of what kind of faith justifies. Remember that the Roman Catholic Church in the sixteenth century taught that faith is necessary for justification. But it maintained that it is possible for a person to have true faith and still not be in a state of justification. The Reformers responded that authentic faith is all that is necessary to be linked to Christ and to be counted just in the sight of

God. So then, a key question concerns the nature of the kind of faith that justifies.

In defense of the Roman Catholic Church, the Roman theologians of the sixteenth century were terrified that some people would hear *justification by faith alone* and think that it means that all a person needs to be saved is a casual acceptance of the truth claims of Christianity, with no accompanying change in the person's life. They were concerned that this formula would open a floodgate of iniquity. So it was imperative for the Reformers to define the character and nature of saving faith. The Reformed theologians discerned ten distinct dimensions to the concept of faith as it is found in the New Testament, which have been condensed to three major aspects of saving faith.

The first aspect of saving faith is *notitia*. It has to do simply with the content of faith, what you believe. How many times have you heard someone say, "It doesn't matter what you believe as long as you're sincere." Maybe you've even said it. What a ghastly thing, to imagine that it doesn't matter what you believe as long as you're sincere! Such a notion is antithetical to the Christian faith. At its heart, Christianity is a body of doctrines that were proclaimed to the world, first by Christ and then His Apostles, that we are called to embrace and to believe. It matters what we believe, and it matters eternally.

Even apart from this idea's incompatibility with the Christian faith, there is this question: What if you're sincerely wrong? Suppose you believe that some inanimate object, like a chair, is the savior of the world. This might seem ridiculous, but it's not that different from what multitudes of people have done throughout history, investing their trust in objects such as statues, totem poles, bushes, or crafted idols. These idols were made by the hands of those who worshiped them, but they actually had faith in their idols. They prayed to them, worshiped them, trusted them to redeem them from the calamities of this world—and they were sincere about it. One of the great tragedies of church history is that heretics tend to be people who are quite sincere in what they believe. Pelagius really believed that Adam's sin did not affect anyone but Adam. Arius really believed that Jesus was not divine. These heretics were sincere in their beliefs, but they were sincerely wrong—and the errors that they taught would doom the world if they were embraced by others.

The Reformers understood that saving faith does not require a perfect understanding of every point of doctrine or systematic theology. We're not justified by knowledge or information alone, but we're also not justified apart from knowledge or information. When the Philippian jailer asked Paul, "What must I do to be saved?" and Paul responded, "Believe in the Lord Jesus, and you will be saved, you and your household" (Acts 16:30–31), that was a bare minimum of content, but there was content there. Paul didn't say to the man, "Believe in the chair you're sitting on," or, "Believe in Baal." He said, "Believe in the Lord Jesus." The preaching of the New Testament sought to condense the essential content of saving faith as the Apostles preached to the world. When they went out to the Gentile communities, they didn't say, "We're going to have a ten-year course on the history of redemption, beginning with the book of Genesis and working up through Malachi. Then we'll ask you to become Christians." No, they had what was called the *kerygma* or "preaching": a summary of the essential claims of the Christian faith, the foundational message of the person and the work of Jesus, the sinfulness of humanity, and the work of reconciliation that had been accomplished by Christ on the cross. That was followed by a call to faith in and commitment to Jesus. As people responded in faith to the *kerygma* and were baptized into the church, they followed up with what was called *didachē* or "teaching," where the whole scope of doctrine was explained in greater detail.

The church in every age has to understand what those essential truths are that we have to grasp in order to be justified. When the Reformers said that one of the necessary ingredients of saving faith is *notitia*, they meant the bare minimum of content that is needed to understand the virgin birth, sinless life, atoning death, and resurrection of Jesus.

That brings up the second essential element of saving faith, which the Reformers called *assensus*. This has to do with agreement or intellectual assent. For Luther and the Reformers, to be justified by faith meant first that you must have the information—*notitia*—and second, you have to believe that the information is true—*assensus*.

Is having those two elements enough to justify you? James told us that it isn't: "You believe that God is one; you do well. Even the demons believe—and shudder!" (James 2:19). Dr. D. James Kennedy of Coral Ridge Presbyterian Church once observed that, if you have only *notitia* and *assensus*, all that does is qualify you to be a demon. The demons were the first to recognize the true character of

Jesus, but they weren't justified. They didn't have saving faith, because the critical element is called *fiducia*, which has to do with trust. So this element of saving faith, so necessary for justification to take place, is one of personal trust and reliance.

In what are you trusting? Upon what are you relying for your reconciliation with God? Many who would say, "Jesus is the Son of God, and did all these wonderful things," when it gets right down to it, are relying on their own performance. "I've tried to live a good life"; "I gave money to those in need"; "I went to church." The object of their faith is themselves, whereas the biblical object of faith is Christ and Him alone. We must put our trust in Him and rely on Him exclusively to be our Redeemer.

Satan and the demons know who Jesus is; they know the truth of the claims of Christ, but Satan would never put his trust in or reliance upon Christ. Why? Because he hates Christ, and because his fundamental sin is pride. He doesn't want to rely on anyone but himself. In order for us to have true faith and trust, we have to see something that Satan doesn't: the loveliness, the sweetness, and the excellence of Christ. We're not going to put trust in someone we despise. But saving faith is quickened in the heart when it understands and embraces the truth of the gospel of Christ and moves from that dimension to personal trust, reliance, and affection for Christ.

Dr. Kennedy once tried to explain *fiducia* using an illustration of a chair. You might look at a chair and see that it doesn't have any defects and so it could probably safely hold you, but you don't truly believe that it can support you until you sit in it. That's the difference between the intellectual aspect of faith and true reliance. Christ is like that chair, and we must risk everything to rest on Him and in Him, recognizing that He alone has the power and the strength to hold us up safely in the presence of God.

Chapter Eight

The Remission of Sins

I used to teach systematic theology and apologetics at seminary. People would often ask me, "What is apologetics?" Briefly stated, apologetics is the science of providing an intellectual and rational defense for the truth claims of Christianity. That necessitates dealing with competing philosophies of the ages. I've been in countless discussions with people, particularly skeptics, trying to give honest answers to their questions and dealing with objections that they raise against Christianity. Often these questions are abstract and philosophical, but I have found that, as these discussions progress, it is virtually inevitable that it comes around to more personal matters. At some point, I ask, "What do you do with your guilt?" Very often when I ask that question, there is a noticeable change in the atmosphere. Not that there's a response of hostility or anger; that hardly ever happens. But there's a sudden soberness that descends, and it's almost palpable.

This is because of the way I ask that question. I don't say, "Do you have guilt?" I don't waste time trying to establish the reality of guilt, because guilt is something of which we are all aware. Guilt is one of the most paralyzing and debilitating forces that attacks humanity, and we try to do all kinds of things about it. One of the most common is denial, but denial cannot work over the long term because no matter how much we deny our guilt, we still have to live with it. We may try to transfer it by shifting the blame to someone else, or we'll seek to rationalize it, putting our sins or guilt in the best possible light.

If I have to answer that question, I only know of one solution to guilt: to have it forgiven. I can't make up for it, deny it, or escape it. My guilt is real, and it's pressing on my life. This is a predicament that we all experience.

This predicament leads us to the most simple and poignant application of justification. The sixteenth-century Reformer John Calvin made this comment: "Now let us examine how true that statement is which is spoken in the definition, that the righteousness of faith is reconciliation with God, which consists solely in the forgiveness of sins." Later in the same paragraph, Calvin concluded, "It is obvious, therefore, that those whom God embraces are made righteous solely by the fact that they are purified when their spots are washed away by forgiveness of sins. Consequently, such righteousness can be called, in a word, 'remission of sins.'"* In this brief paragraph, Calvin says that the way we are made righteous or justified before God is through having our sins forgiven, which ultimately consists solely in this: the remission of sins.

One context where we hear the term *remission* used is the medical world. Those who have been afflicted with cancer, having undergone surgery or treatment, then rejoice to hear the good news that their malignancy is "in remission." Another context where we encounter the term is related to bills: if you owe money to a store, for example, they'll state

---

* *Institutes* 3.11.21.

at the bottom of the bill, "Please remit payment with this return envelope." When you send in your money to pay your bill, you've engaged in the remission of funds.

These may seem to be quite different uses of the term *remission*, but there is a point of contact between the two. Cancer that has gone into remission has, at least for the time being, gone away. When you pay your bills, you send your money away as you remit it. Taking those usages from common language and applying them over to the realm of theology, we already get a sense of what is meant when we talk about the remission of sins. The remission of sins in our justification occurs when God sends our guilt away; He removes it from us "as far as the east is from the west" (Ps. 103:12).

In the first chapter of Isaiah, God makes an appeal through the prophet: "Come now, let us reason together, says the LORD" (v. 18). He was inviting His people to come near. For what purpose? To reason together, to apply their minds to have an understanding of the problem. It is the people's guilt that precipitates the invitation. He added this to this invitation: "Though your sins are like scarlet, they shall be white as snow; though they are red like crimson, they shall become like wool." Scarlet is an exceedingly deep and rich shade of the color red. Sin is like a stain that no amount of scrubbing can remove, yet God promises to get it cleaner than we can imagine, so clean that you'd never know the stain was there.

When my daughter became a Christian, we were at a Presbyterian church in Ohio, and she was just in grade school. At one evening service, we had a guest minister, and my daughter went to a special program they offered for children. At the end of this service, the minister made an invitation for those who wanted to commit their lives to Christ to come forward—an unusual procedure in Presbyterian churches, but they did this once a year at this particular church. I was standing in the chancel and watching the adults moving forward when, to my utter astonishment, I saw my own daughter parading down the center of the aisle. I thought, "She's too young to be doing this; this is just an emotional thing." I was concerned, so afterward I asked her what moved her to come forward. "Daddy, I had to," she said. "I just couldn't sit still." I asked, "How do you feel about it?" She said, "I just feel clean, like a newborn baby." I thought that was a remarkable understanding of the experience of forgiveness for a six-year-old girl.

One of the most famous sermons in the New Testament was delivered by the Apostle Peter on the day of Pentecost. In the second chapter of Acts, we read this account:

> But Peter, standing with the eleven, lifted up his voice and addressed them: "Men of Judea and all who dwell in Jerusalem, let this be known to you, and give ear to my words. For these people are not drunk, as you suppose, since it is only the third hour of the day. . . . Men of Israel, hear these words: Jesus of Nazareth, a man attested to you by God with mighty works and wonders and signs that God did through him in your midst, as you yourselves know—this Jesus, delivered up according to the definite plan and foreknowledge of God, you crucified and killed by the hands of lawless men. God raised him up, loosing the pangs of death, because it was not possible for him to be held by it." (Acts 2:14–15, 22–24).

Often the objection is raised against the resurrection of Christ that it's simply impossible. One thing that we know for sure is that, when a person dies, he stays dead; it's just not credible to put your confidence in the resurrection, because a resurrection is impossible. Yet Peter declared that it was not possible for Christ to stay dead—He was a sinless man, and death is the punishment for sin. It was not possible for death to hold Christ in its grip for any length of time. He concluded the sermon this way:

> "Let all the house of Israel therefore know for certain that God has made him both Lord and Christ, this Jesus whom you crucified." Now when they heard this they were cut to the heart, and said to Peter and the rest of the apostles, "Brothers, what shall we do?" And Peter said to them, "Repent and be baptized every one of you in the name of Jesus Christ for the forgiveness of your sins, and you will receive the gift of the Holy Spirit. For the promise is for you and for your children and for all who are far off, everyone whom the Lord our God calls to himself." (vv. 36–39)

Five thousand people or so were added to the church on that day, and we are told that when Peter gave this message, the response of the people was one of acute awareness of guilt. "What shall we do?" they asked. Maybe you've experienced that excruciating stabbing of the conscience. Peter answered the question saying, "Repent and be baptized every one of you in the name of Jesus Christ for the forgiveness of your sins." Do you see the sequence? Repentance, then remission. It's as true today as it was then: the essence of justification, the only relief for those who are burdened by the reality of guilt, is the remission of sins—and that remission is available, and will be received instantly to all who genuinely repent.

Perhaps these things, in the providence of God, were specifically for your benefit. I don't know who reads these books, but I know that all of us face the problem of relief from guilt; if there's anything that applies to all of us, it is the need for the remission of our sins. Just like David, when he was brought to a state of contrition and repentance as he wrote in Psalm 51, cried out, "Have mercy on me, O God, according to your steadfast love; according to your abundant mercy blot out my transgressions" (v. 1). What was he saying? "O God, send them away! Erase them from Your record."

Chapter Nine

Peace with God

As Luther emphasized, justification is the doctrine upon which the church stands or falls. But if the doctrine makes no difference in our lives, it's in danger of remaining a matter of abstract theology. The remaining question, then, is: So what? What is the benefit of having been justified? What is the fruit of that justification?

Let's turn our attention to the fifth chapter of Paul's letter to the Romans. In chapters 3 and 4, Paul gives us the most in-depth exposition of the doctrine of justification anywhere in his writings; chapter 5 begins with this word: "therefore." Anytime you see "therefore" in Scripture, it should pique your attention. What does the word "therefore" indicate? It's the word that precedes a conclusion. Paul spent two chapters defining and explaining justification, and then he presents a conclusion: "Therefore, since we have been justified by faith. . . ." Paul speaks about something that has already been accomplished—he writes to those in Rome as people who were in a state of justification. "Since we have been justified by faith, we have peace with God through our Lord Jesus Christ" (v. 1). That's the first result of justification.

How important was that message to an ancient Jew, whose concern for peace in every dimension was monumental? Peace was so important to the Jews that they greeted people with the word *shalom*—peace. When Jews would meet or depart, they said the same greeting: *Shalom aleichem, aleichem shalom*—"Peace be to you, and unto you, peace." What kind of peace were they looking for? Of course, they wanted peace from the endless warfare that besieged their nation, which had had less than a hundred years' peace in its whole history. Also, they longed for that inner peace—tranquility, rest of the soul—that all people desperately want and seek in this world. But the ultimate peace is to have reconciliation with the supreme enemy of their existence.

Do you realize that the most formidable opponent that you've ever had in your life—your most hostile enemy, the most threatening alien to your well-being—is Almighty God? Sometimes people look at me quizzically when I say that. Many people think of God as some sort of celestial grandfather, a cosmic bellhop, who loves everyone and who is so gracious and merciful that He could never really be someone's enemy. But that's not what the New Testament teaches. Again and again, the Bible describes the relationship between a holy God and unholy people as a relationship of estrangement. The Scripture teaches us that, by nature, we are at enmity with God; we are the mortal enemies of our Creator, and our relationship with God is defined in terms of estrangement. Therefore, the central motif of all of Scripture is the concept of reconciliation. Christ is called the "Mediator" between God and us. But if there's no estrangement, there's no need for reconciliation; if there's no conflict, there's no need for a mediator. We've somehow cheapened the message of the New Testament to such a degree that we've all but forgotten that there was a problem in the first place.

The New Testament takes that problem very seriously, and Paul wrote that the key to reconciliation—the end of conflict between the sinner and God, the truce that is declared—comes with our justification. Those who are not in a state of justification are in a war to the finish with their Creator. They are alienated and estranged from Him if they are not justified. But for those who are justified—who have repented, bowed the knee to Christ, and put confidence in Him alone as Redeemer and Mediator—the good news is that they have peace with God.

One day in my childhood, I was playing stickball on the streets of Chicago when the game was interrupted by a sudden melee that broke out. Adults came running out of apartment buildings, shops, and stores, screaming and yelling and pounding on pots and pans. I was frightened and surprised, and I was irritated that the game was interrupted. The people were shouting and screaming, "It's over! It's over!" It was V-J Day, 1945. The horrible conflict of World War II was over. I remember even as a child experiencing a flood of relief, because I knew at least in existential terms that this meant my father could come home and be with us, safe at last.

One of the scariest moments of my life as an eight- or

nine-year-old was when I was invited by some of the guys in the neighborhood to spend the night sleeping out in a tent, and as we were getting ready to go to sleep, one of the guys started talking about the atomic bomb. We had had exercises in school to practice for air raid alerts in the event of a nuclear attack. This older fellow was telling us how destructive the atomic bomb was, and how, in his judgment, it was inevitable that one was going to fall sooner or later. I became so frightened that I left the tent and came home. I was sick to my stomach, and I remember living on the edge of fear that another war would come about. In this world, peace treaties are established, but they've never been the true end of war. All of our truces in this world are guarded truces; at any moment, hostilities can break out again and the domestic tranquility be thrown into upheaval anew.

That is not the case with God. When we are justified, we have peace with God that is forever. It's not a guarded peace or an uneasy truce. God is not going to start rattling a saber every time we offend or disobey Him after we have received the grace of justification. The peace that belongs inherently to Christ is given to us when we put our faith in Him. Do you remember the last will and testament of Jesus? He gave it to His disciples before He died when He said, "Let not your hearts be troubled. Believe in God; believe also in me" (John 14:1). He said, "In my Father's house are many rooms. If it were not so, would I have told you that I go to prepare a place for you? And if I go and prepare a place for you, I will come again and will take you to myself, that where I am you may be also" (vv. 2–3). Then what did He say? "Peace I leave with you; my peace I give to you. Not as the world gives do I give to you. Let not your hearts be troubled, neither let them be afraid" (v. 27). When Christ, as the Mediator, paid the price for our sins—and when God declares us just in Christ—the war is over, and it's over forever.

My wife once asked me, "Does God ever punish Christians for their sins?" I said, "Certainly He does. The Scriptures tell us that the Lord chastises, rebukes, admonishes, and chastens us—but it also says that the Lord chastens those whom He loves." It is not punitive wrath that we receive from the Father, but corrective wrath; it is the discipline that a loving Father gives to His children. But there is no end to the peace. We can disappoint God, disobey Him, offend Him, or grieve Him—but we will never again be estranged from God, because having been justified, we have our reconciliation and our Mediator who intercedes for us all the time, who has made absolutely certain that the war is finished and there will be no more war between us and God. Paul said, "Therefore, since we have been justified by faith, we have peace with God through our Lord Jesus Christ. Through him we have also obtained access by faith into this grace in which we stand, and we rejoice in hope of the glory of God" (Rom. 5:1–2). So the first fruit of justification is peace.

The second is access. The whole history of Israel had changed, according to Paul. After the first sin, Adam and Eve were banished from paradise and forced to live east of Eden; the gateway to paradise was guarded by an angel with a flaming sword. There would be no access to the presence of God. Through the history of Old Testament Israel, the place of meeting between God and His people—first in the tabernacle, then in the temple—had at its core the *sanctus sanctorum*: the Holy of Holies. No ordinary person was allowed ever to set foot there; the only one allowed into the Holy of Holies was the high priest, and then only once a year after elaborate ceremonies and rites of purification. For the rest of the people, there was no access to the immediate presence of God, a fact that was symbolized by a huge, heavy veil or curtain that separated the Holy Place from the Holy of Holies.

But on the day that Christ gave His atonement for sin, what happened in the temple? An earthquake struck, and the veil in the temple was torn in two; the barrier that God had erected between Himself and His people was removed because of Christ. Because He has made us just in the sight of God, we have peace; we have access. The author of Hebrews wrote, "Therefore, brothers, since we have confidence to enter the holy places by the blood of Jesus, by the new and living way that he opened for us through the curtain, that is, through his flesh, and since we have a great priest over the house of God, let us draw near with a true heart in full assurance of faith, with our hearts sprinkled clean from an evil conscience and our bodies washed with pure water" (Heb. 10:19–22). The Old Testament believer would have suffered death if he had just touched the holy mountain of Sinai; now God says, "Come—enter into My presence." We are to come boldly into the presence of God, because we have access to God by the grace of Christ in which we stand. Remember what the psalmist asked? "If you, O LORD, should mark iniquities, O Lord, who could stand?" (Ps. 130:3).

If you're not justified, there is no way you can stand. But those who have peace with God, having been justified by faith in the finished work of Christ, have access into that grace, into His presence, in which we now stand. That is the supreme privilege granted to the believer by God's grace alone through faith alone in Christ alone.

About the Author

Dr. R.C. Sproul was founder of Ligonier Ministries, founding pastor of Saint Andrew's Chapel in Sanford, Fla., first president of Reformation Bible College, and executive editor of *Tabletalk* magazine. His radio program, *Renewing Your Mind*, is still broadcast daily on hundreds of radio stations around the world and can also be heard online. He was author of more than one hundred books, including *The Holiness of God, Chosen by God,* and *Everyone's a Theologian*. He was recognized throughout the world for his articulate defense of the inerrancy of Scripture and the need for God's people to stand with conviction upon His Word.